Angel Aspects

Greyscale and Line Colouring

Morgan Fitzsimons

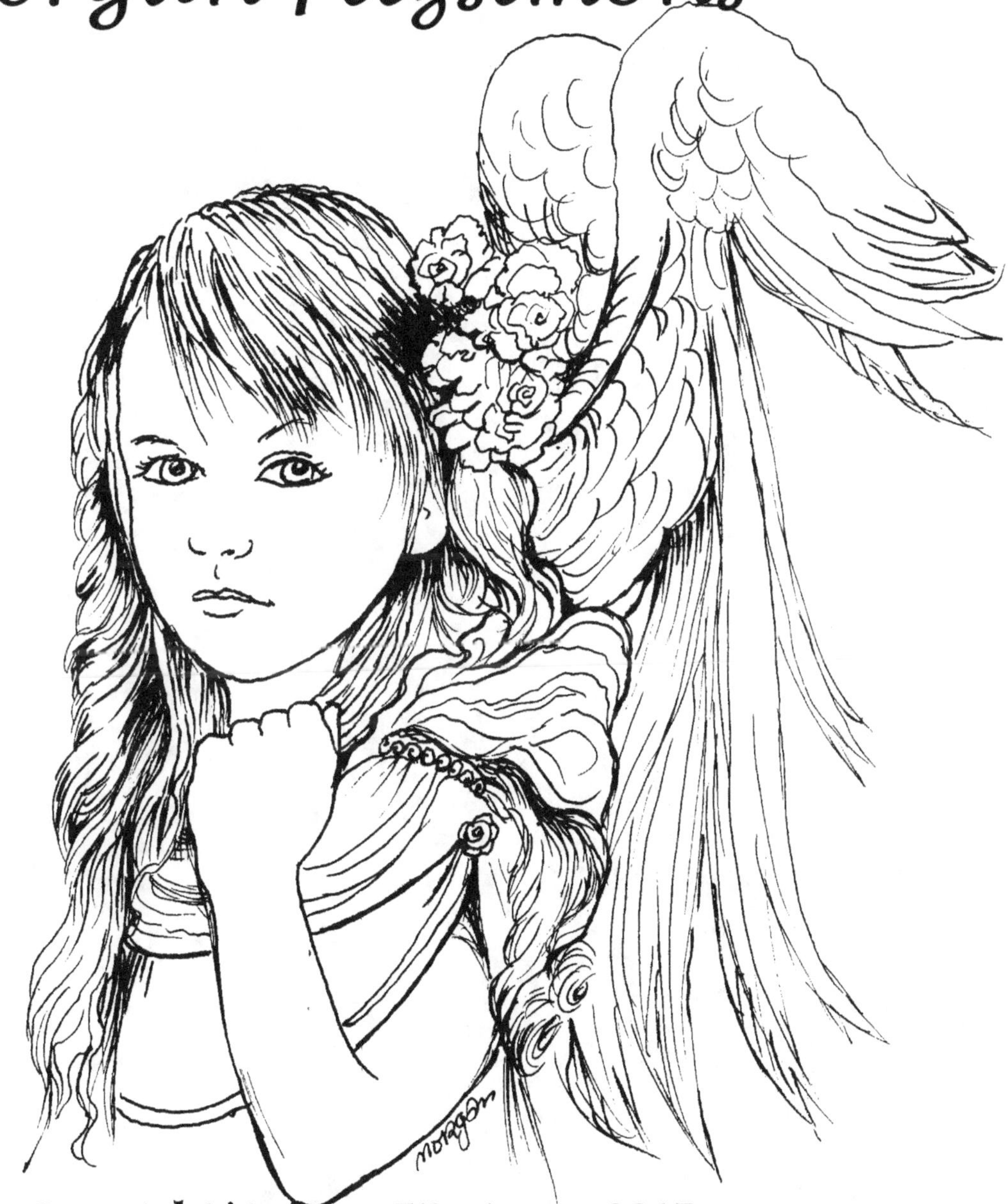

Angel Aspects Colouring Book

Artwork By
Morgan Fitzsimons Author-Artist

Graphics Layout By
Linda Larson

Published by Fae Entertainment & Fae Workshop

ISBN #978 0 9948768-4-3

Published and Printed in All Countries Worldwide

Printed in Paperback

info@Fae-Entertainment.ca

www.MorganFitzsimons.com

www.FaeEntertainment.com

www.Fae-Entertainment.ca

www.ArtStampsStore.com

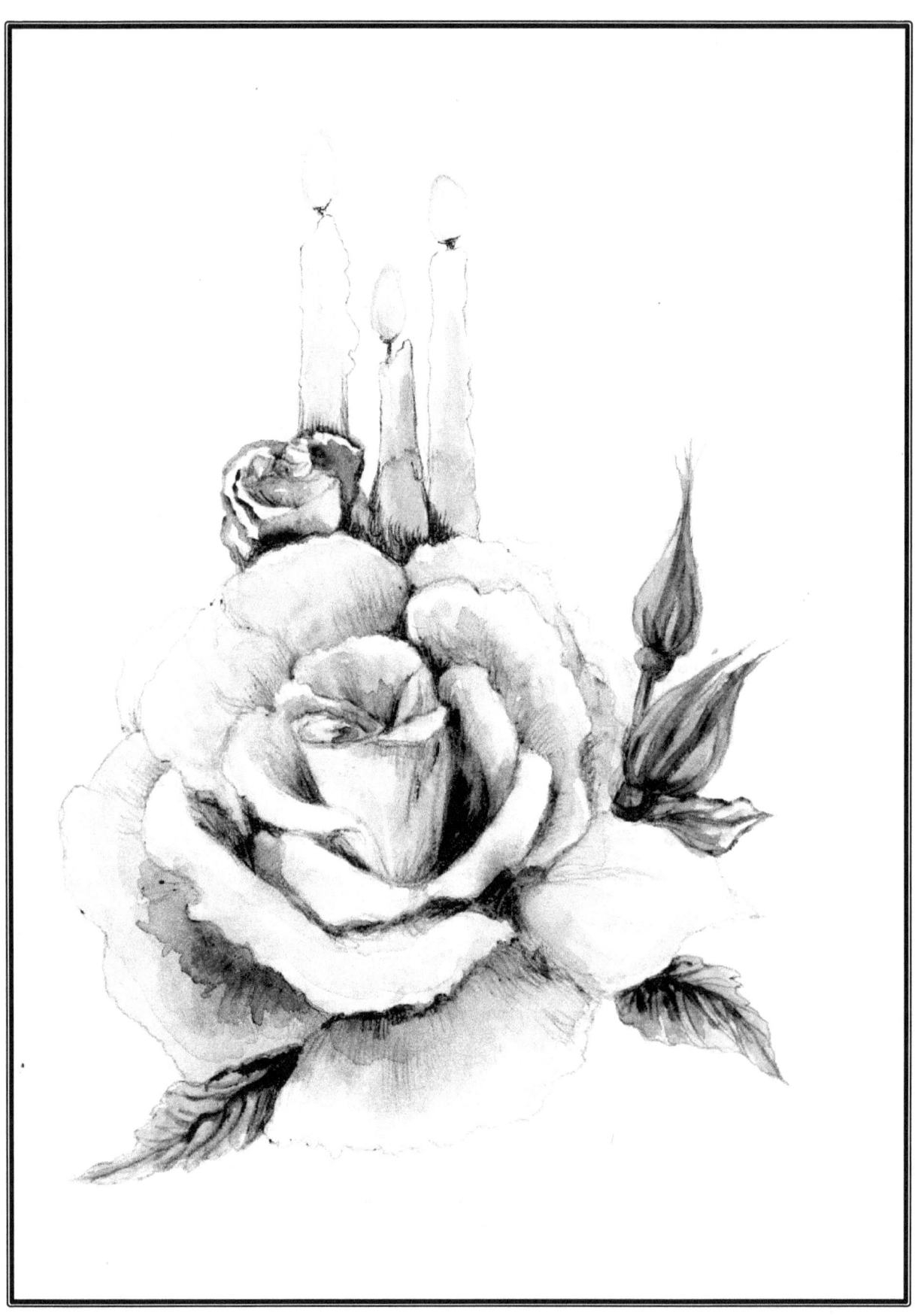

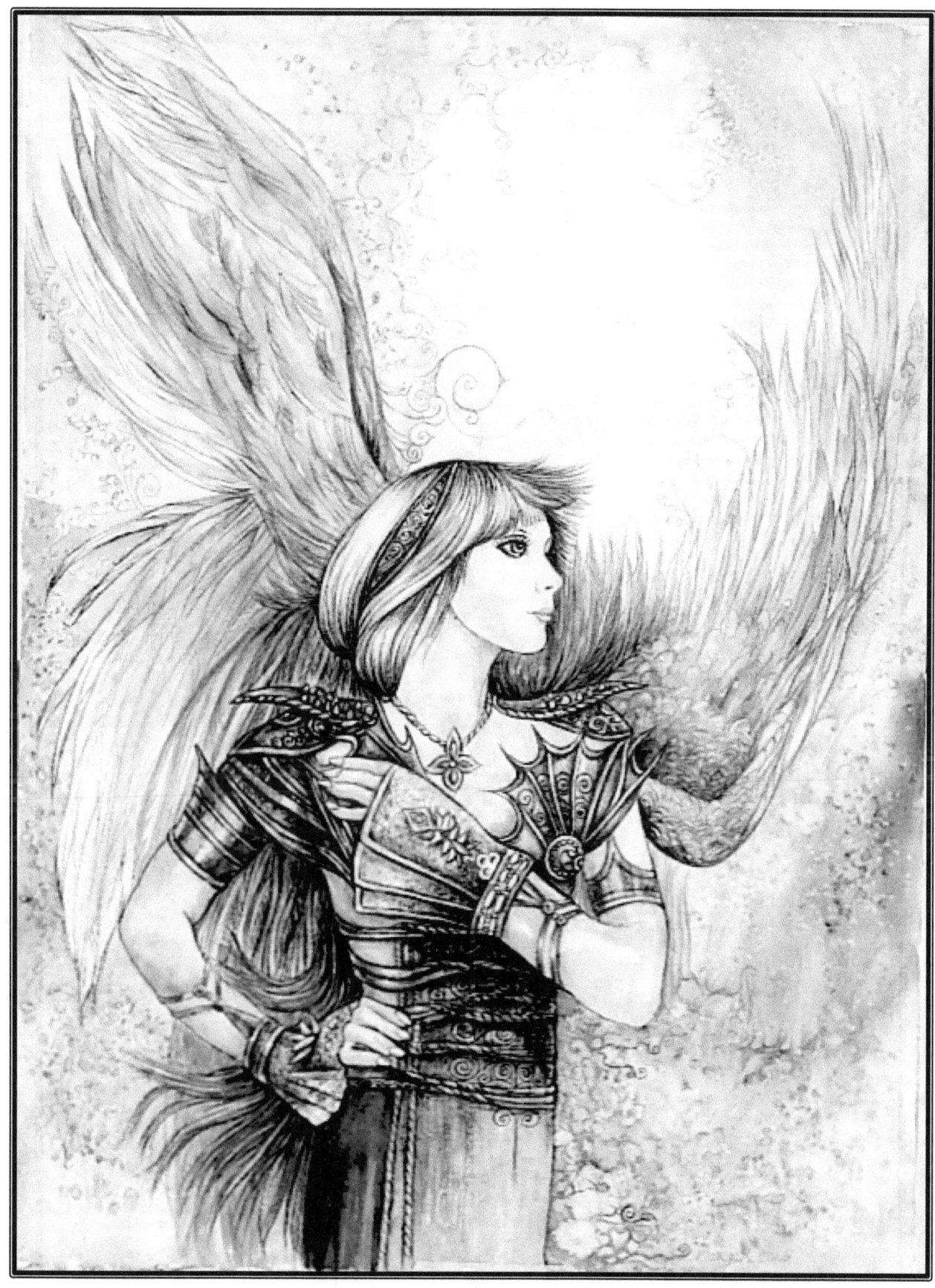

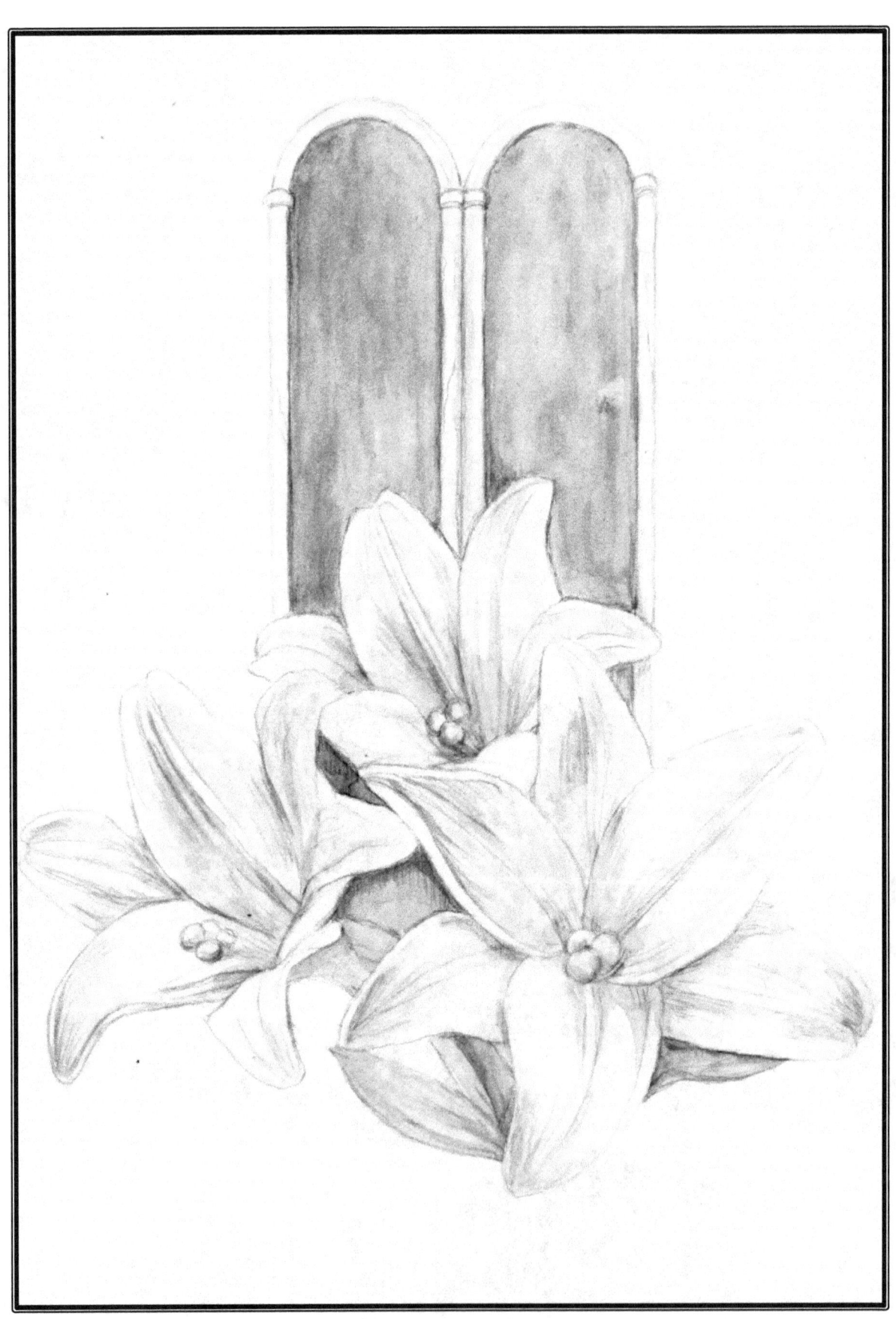

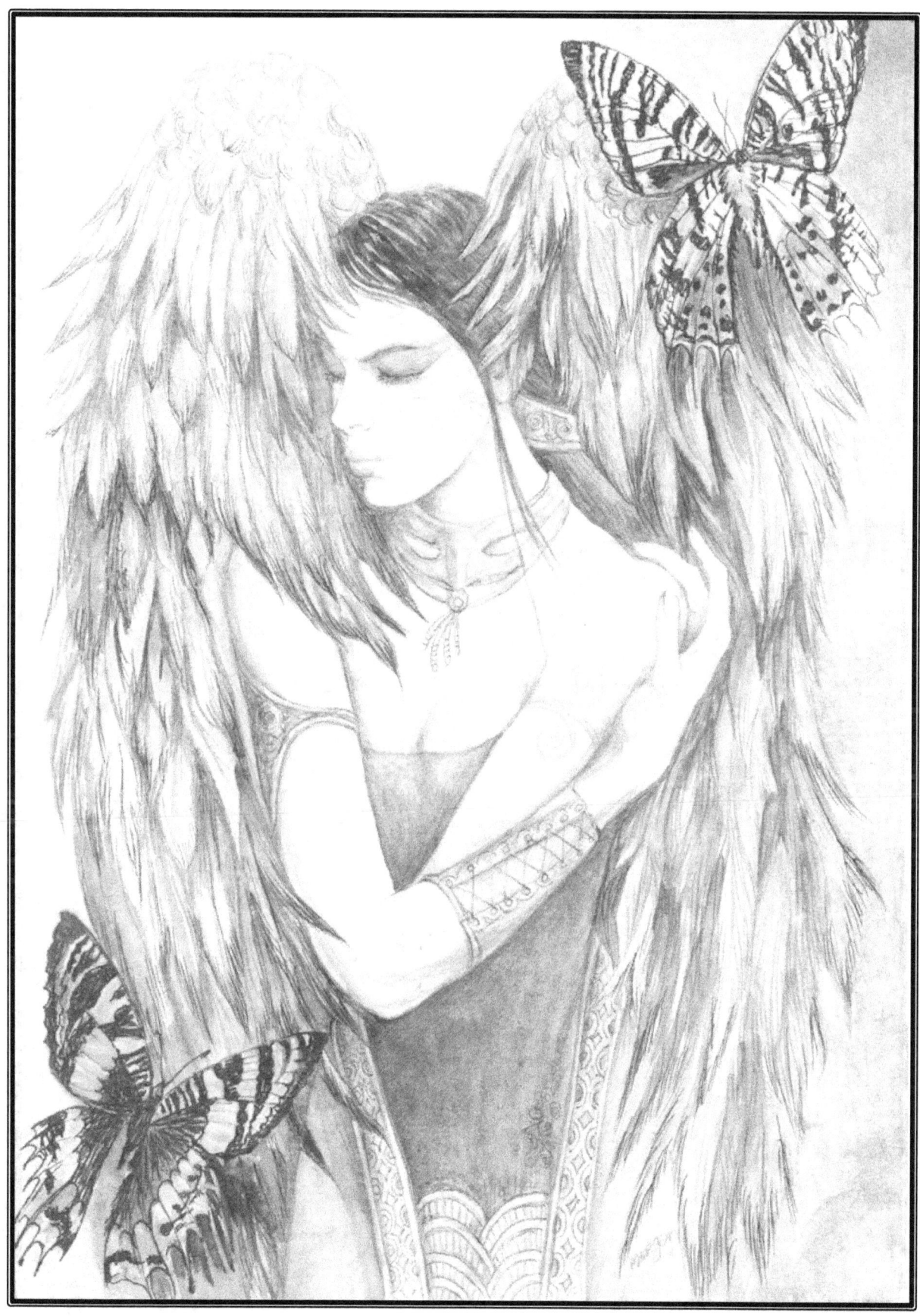

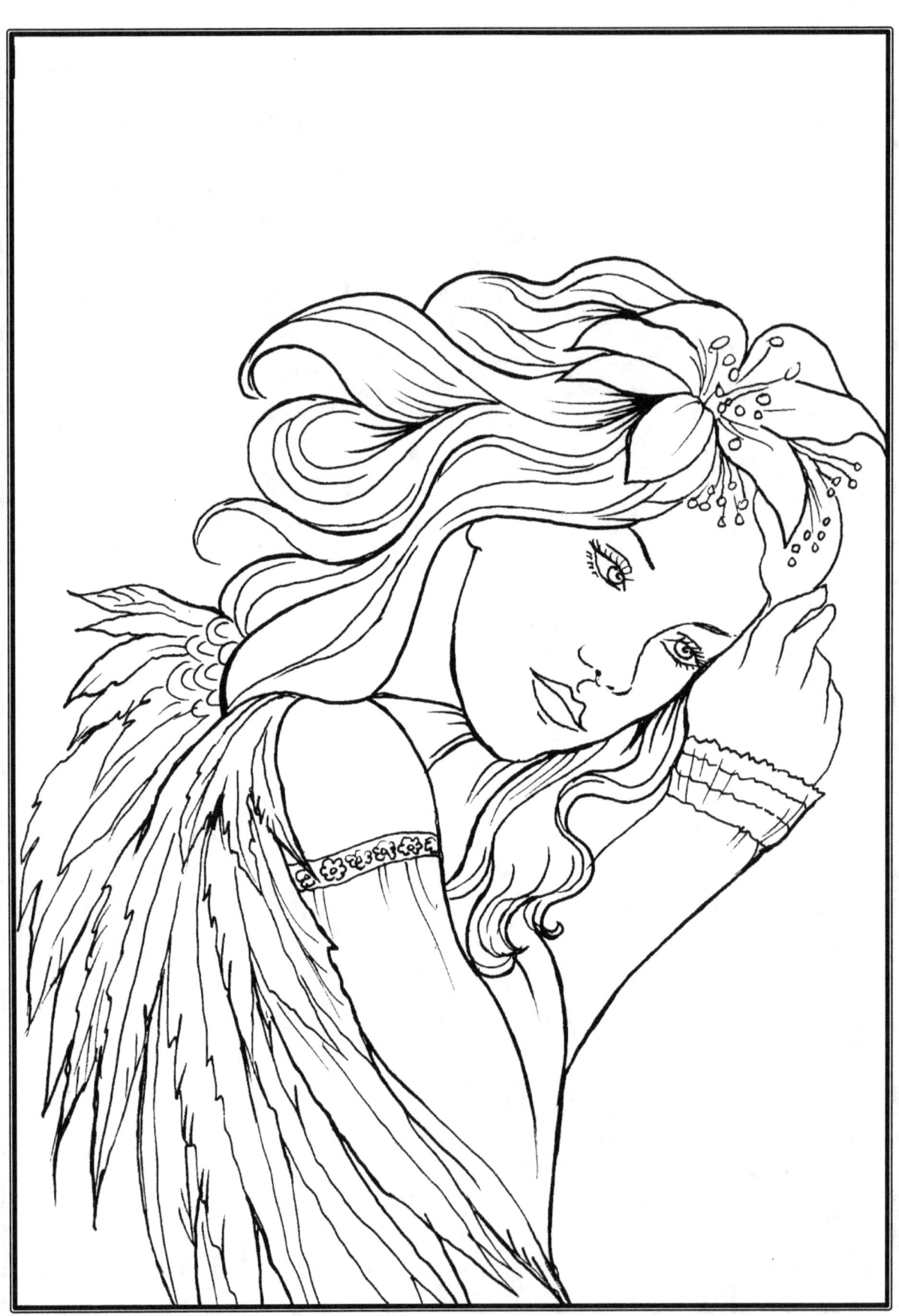

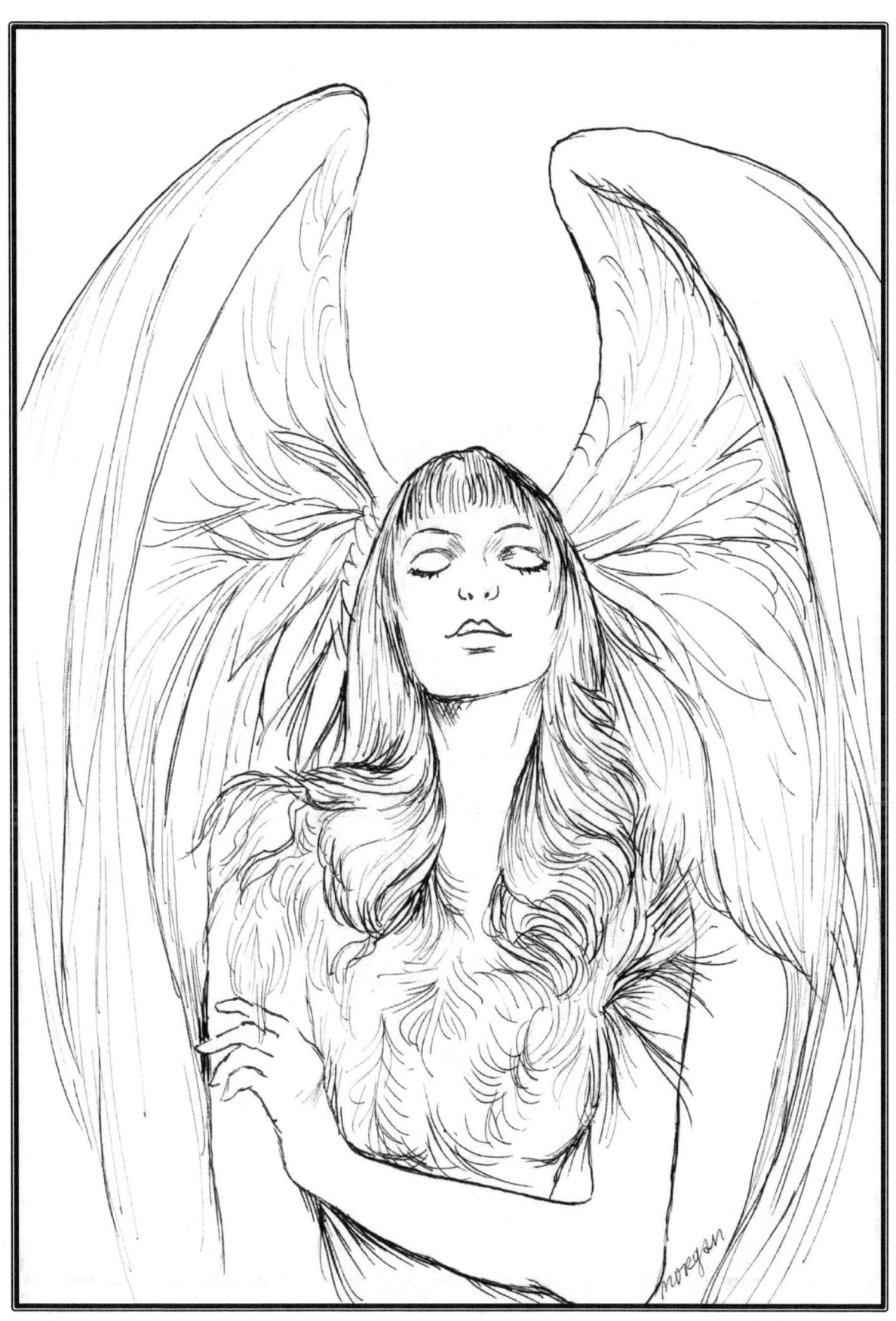

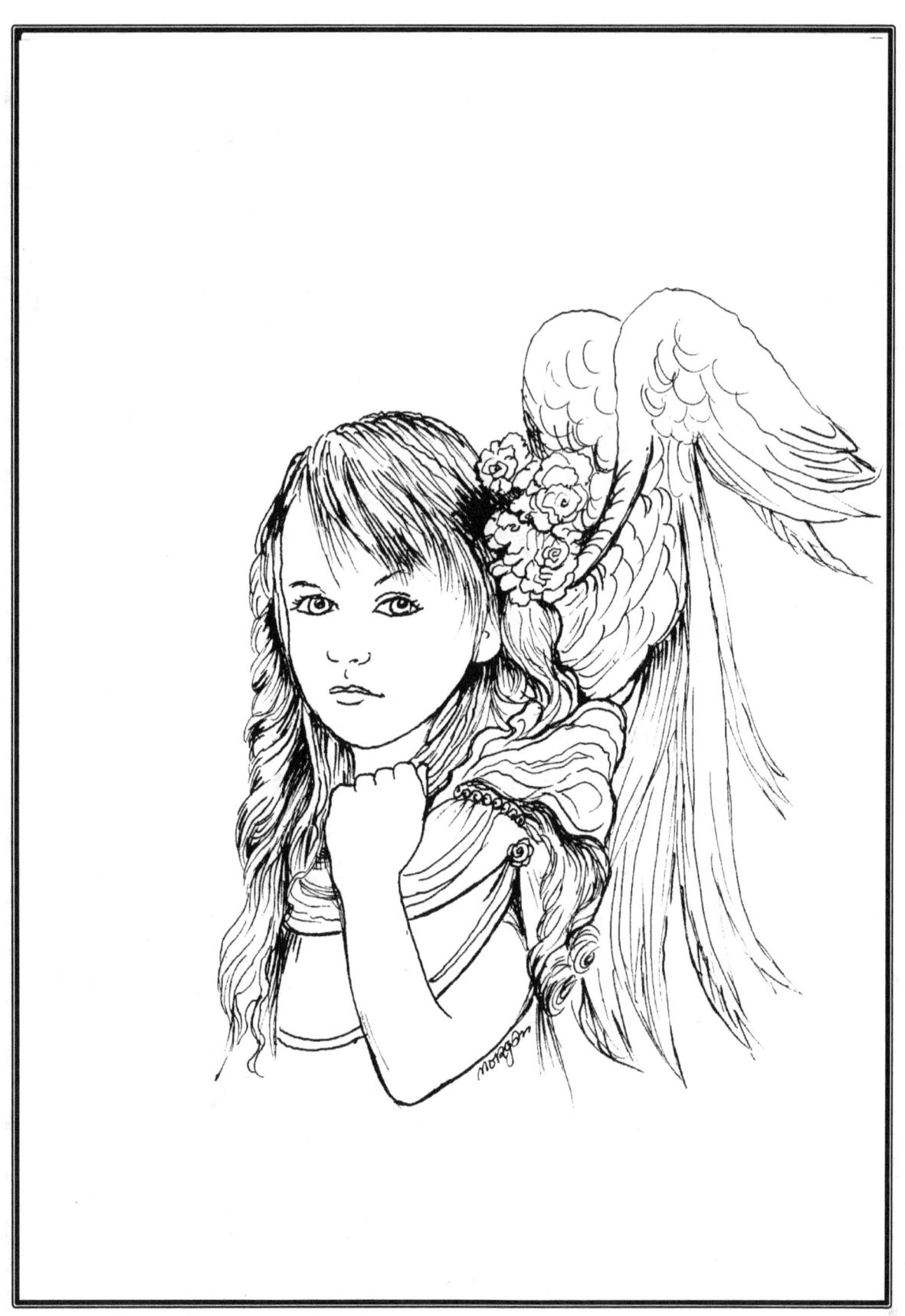

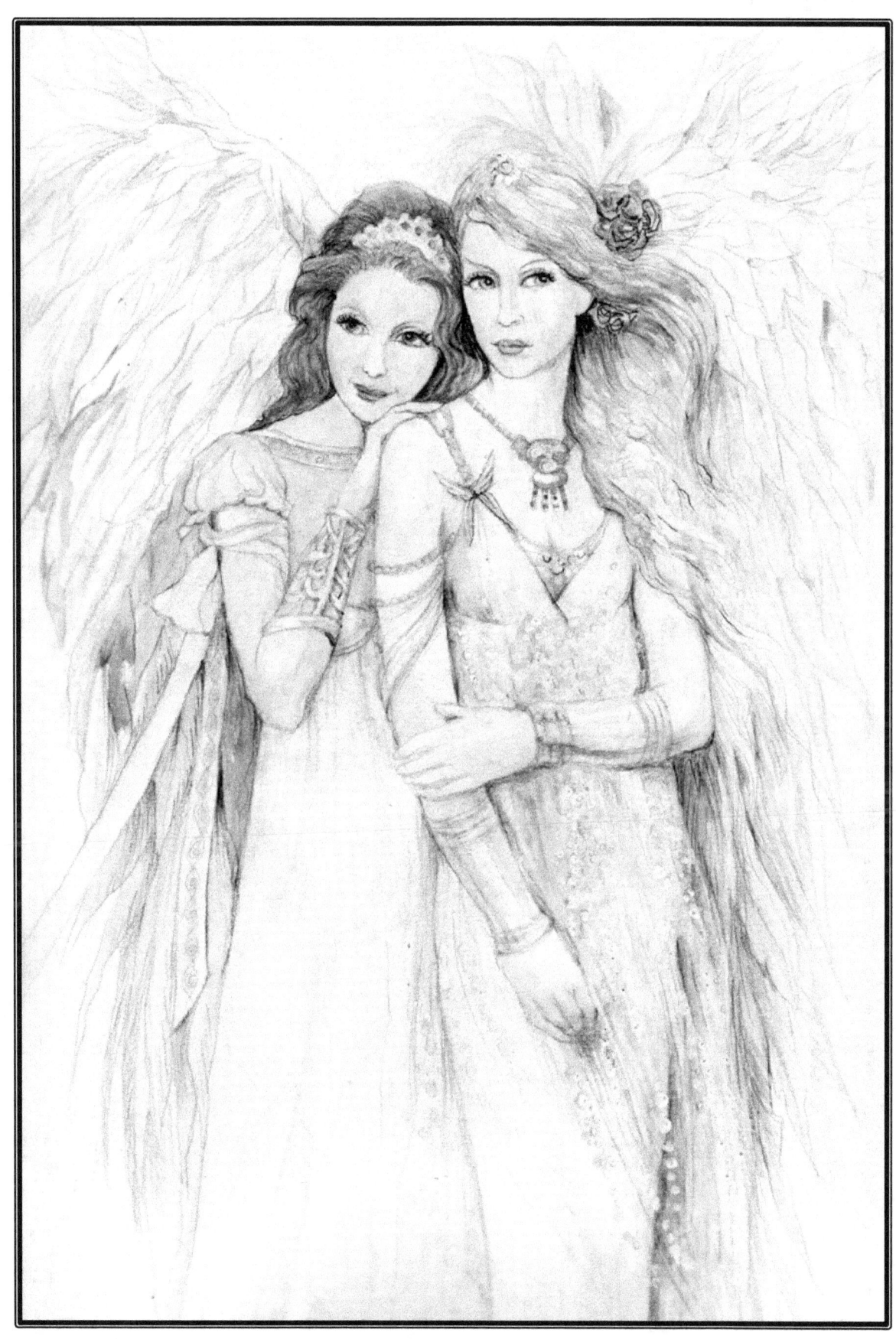

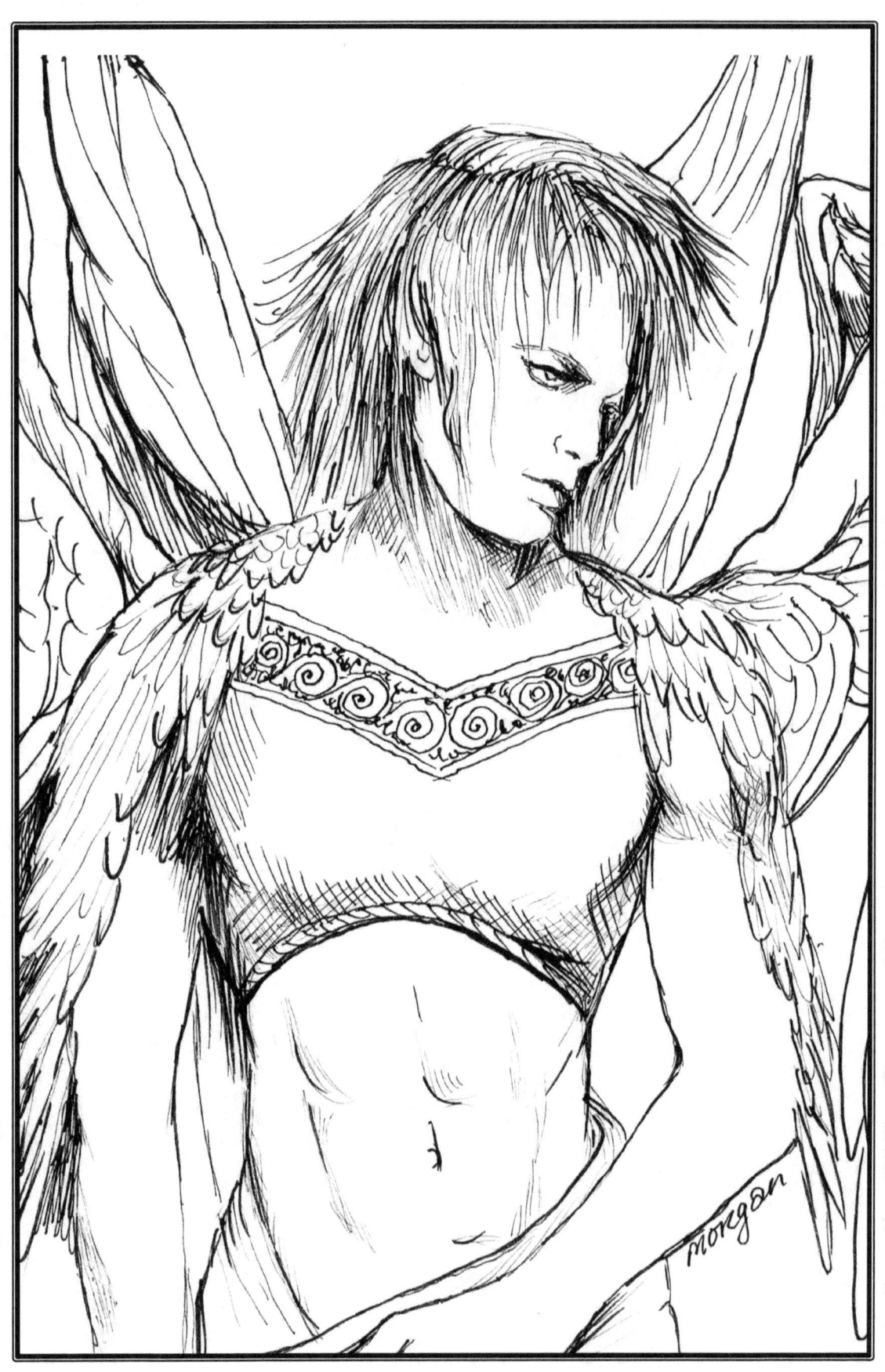

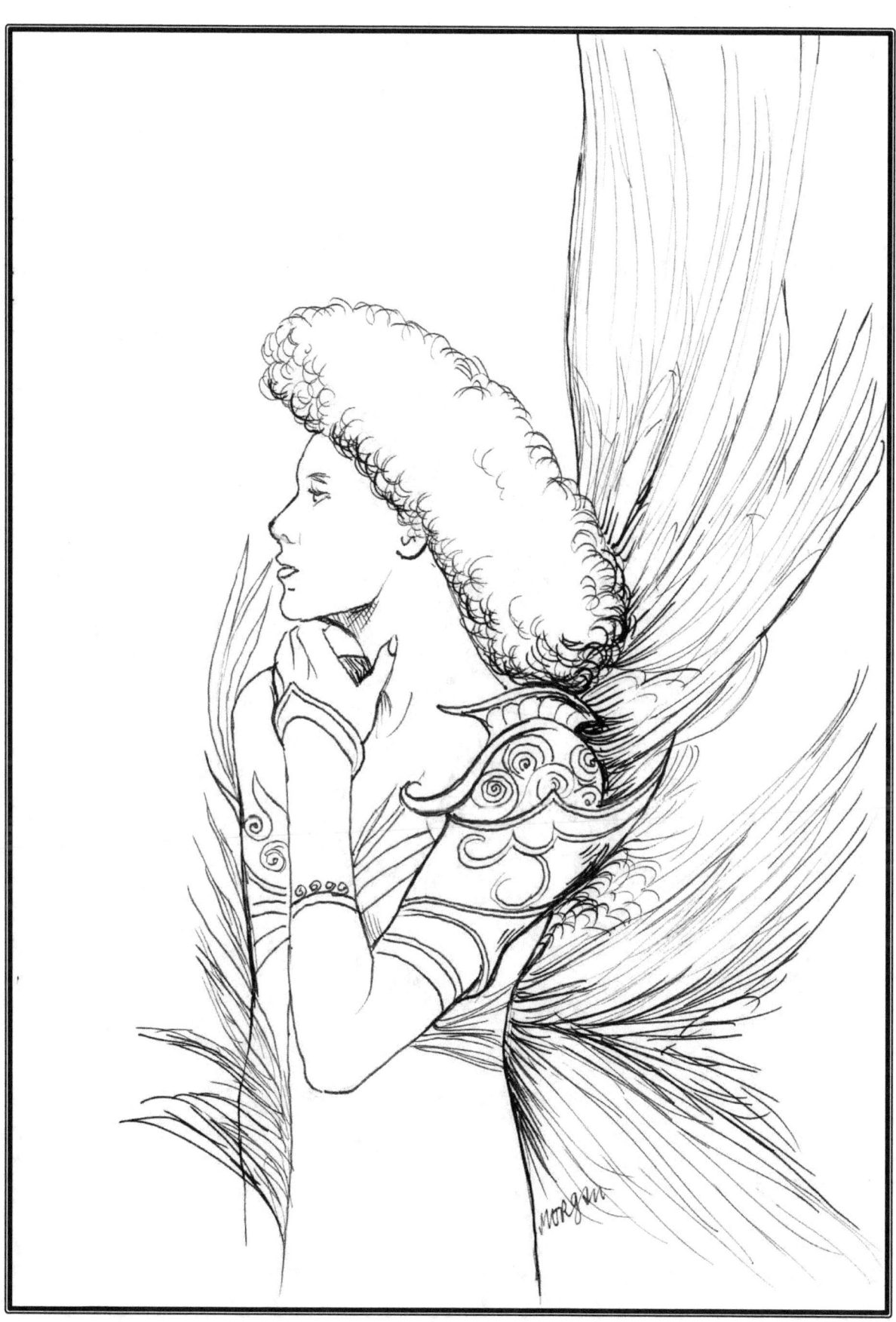

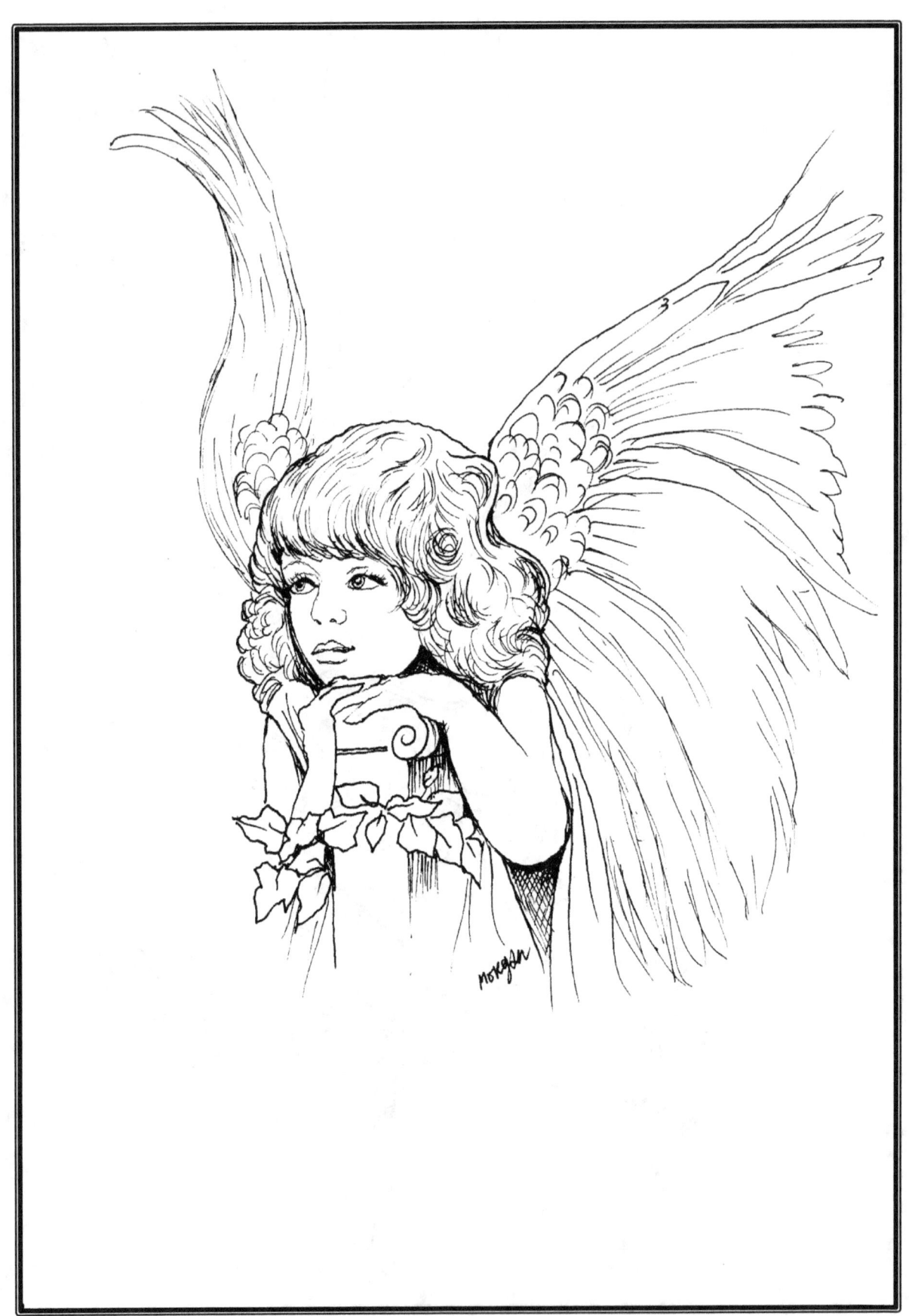

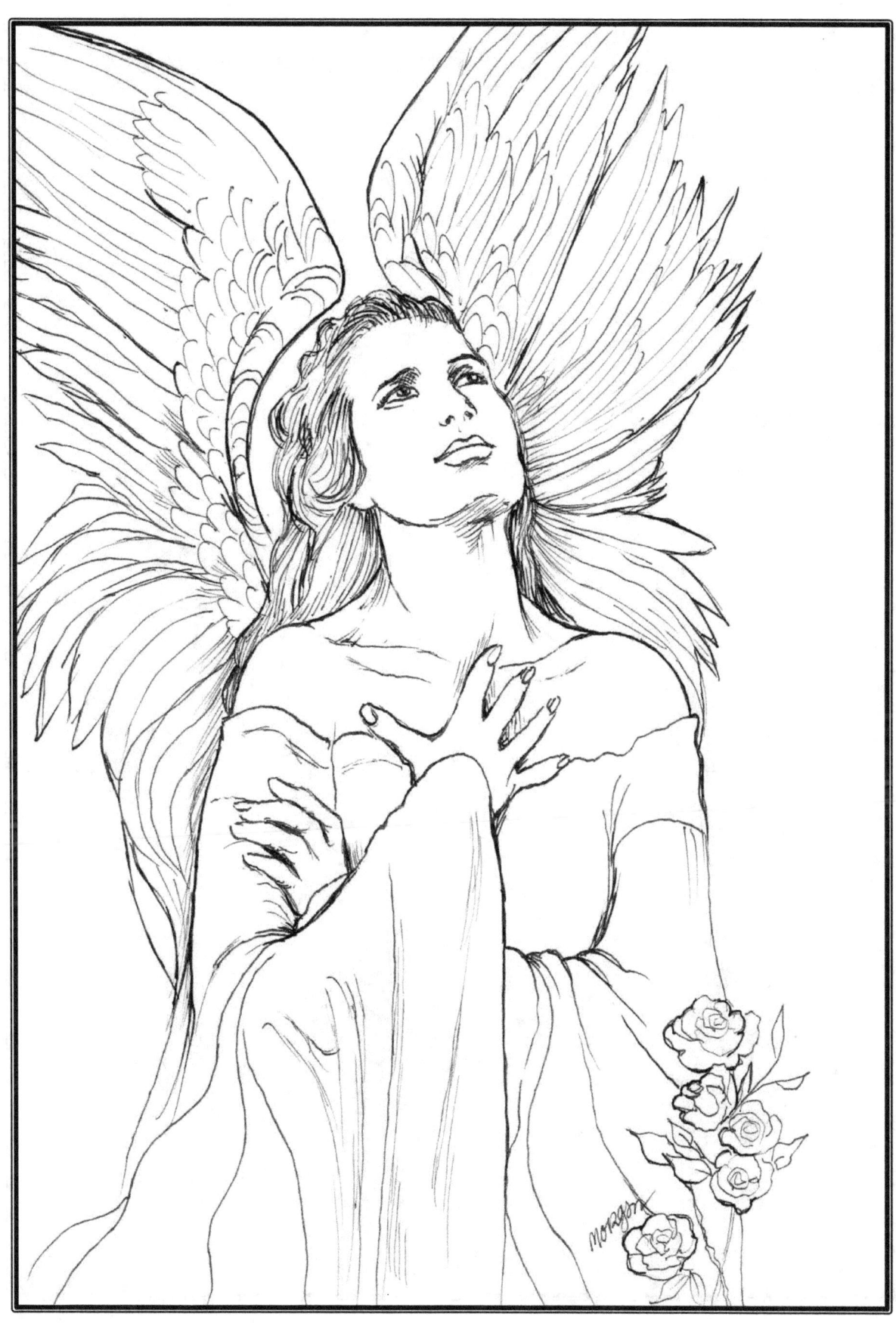

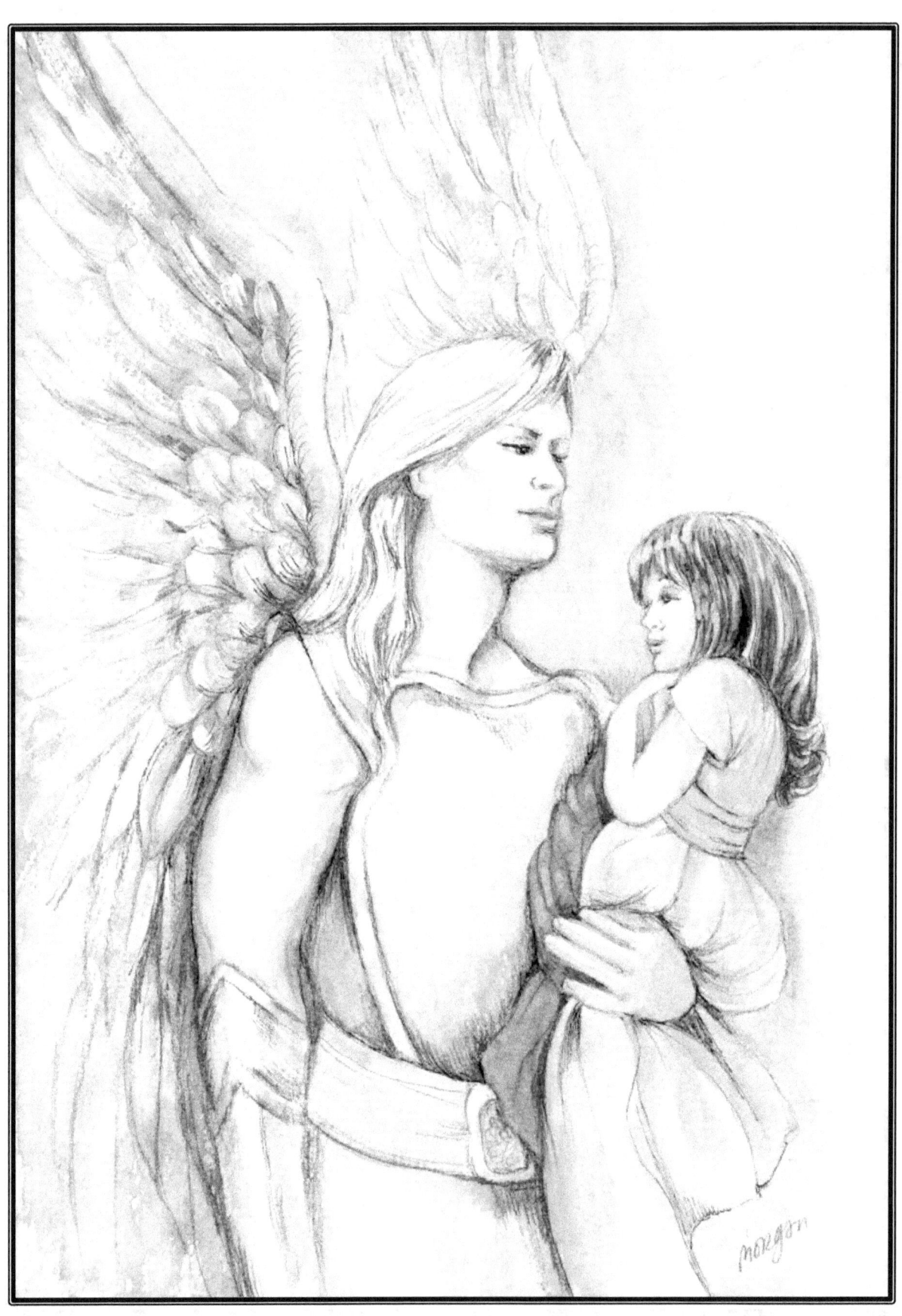

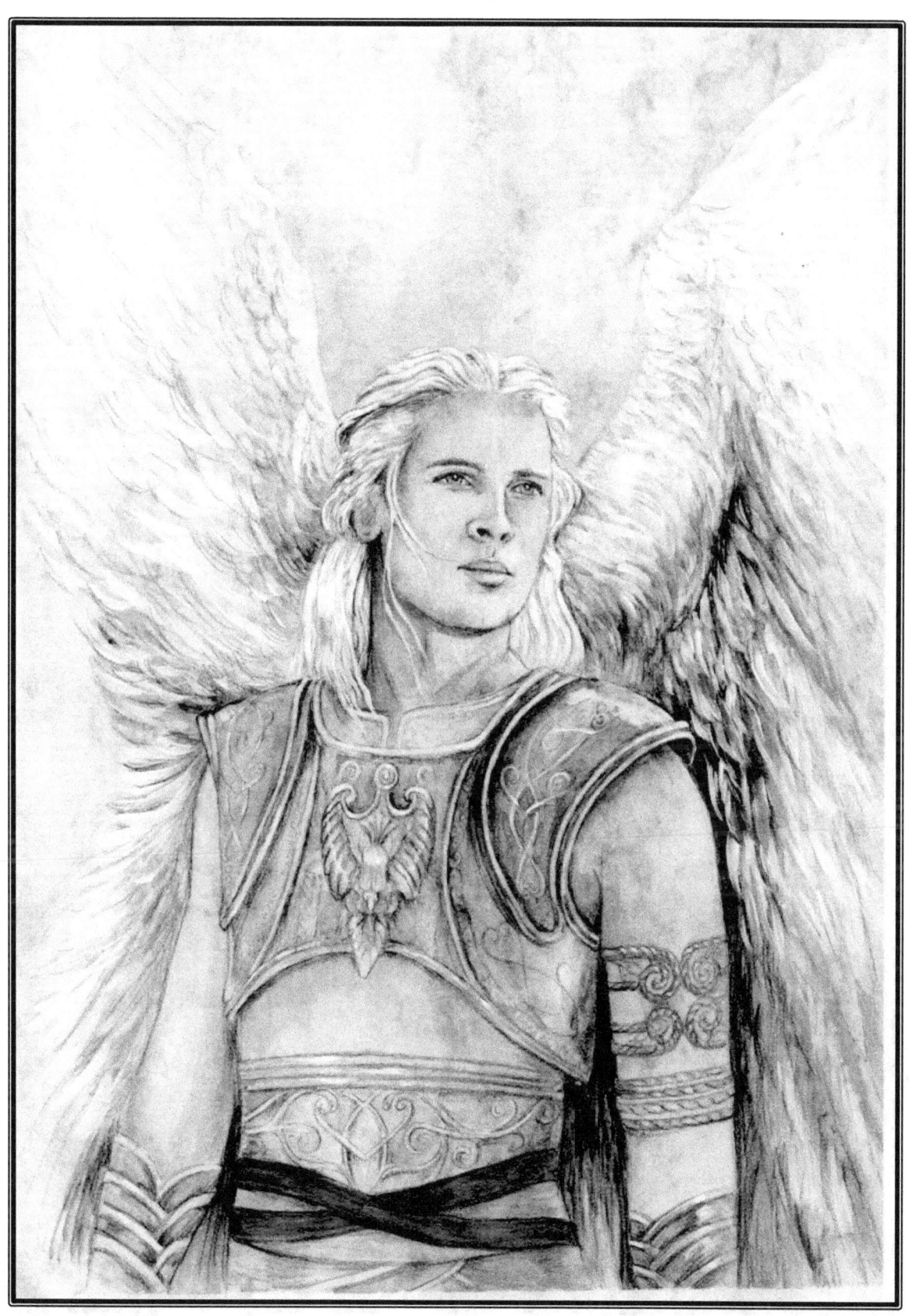

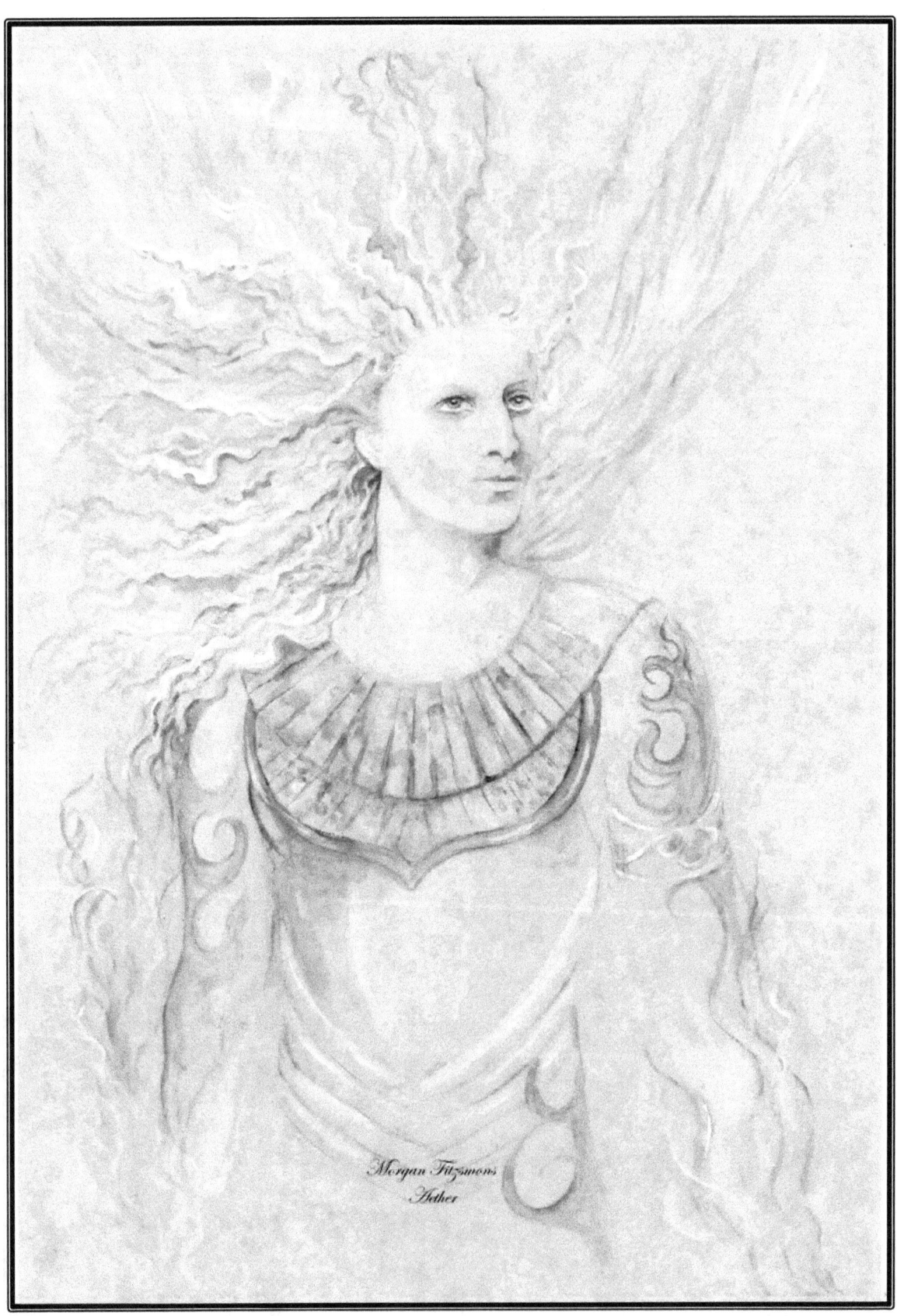

Morgan Fitzsimons
Aether

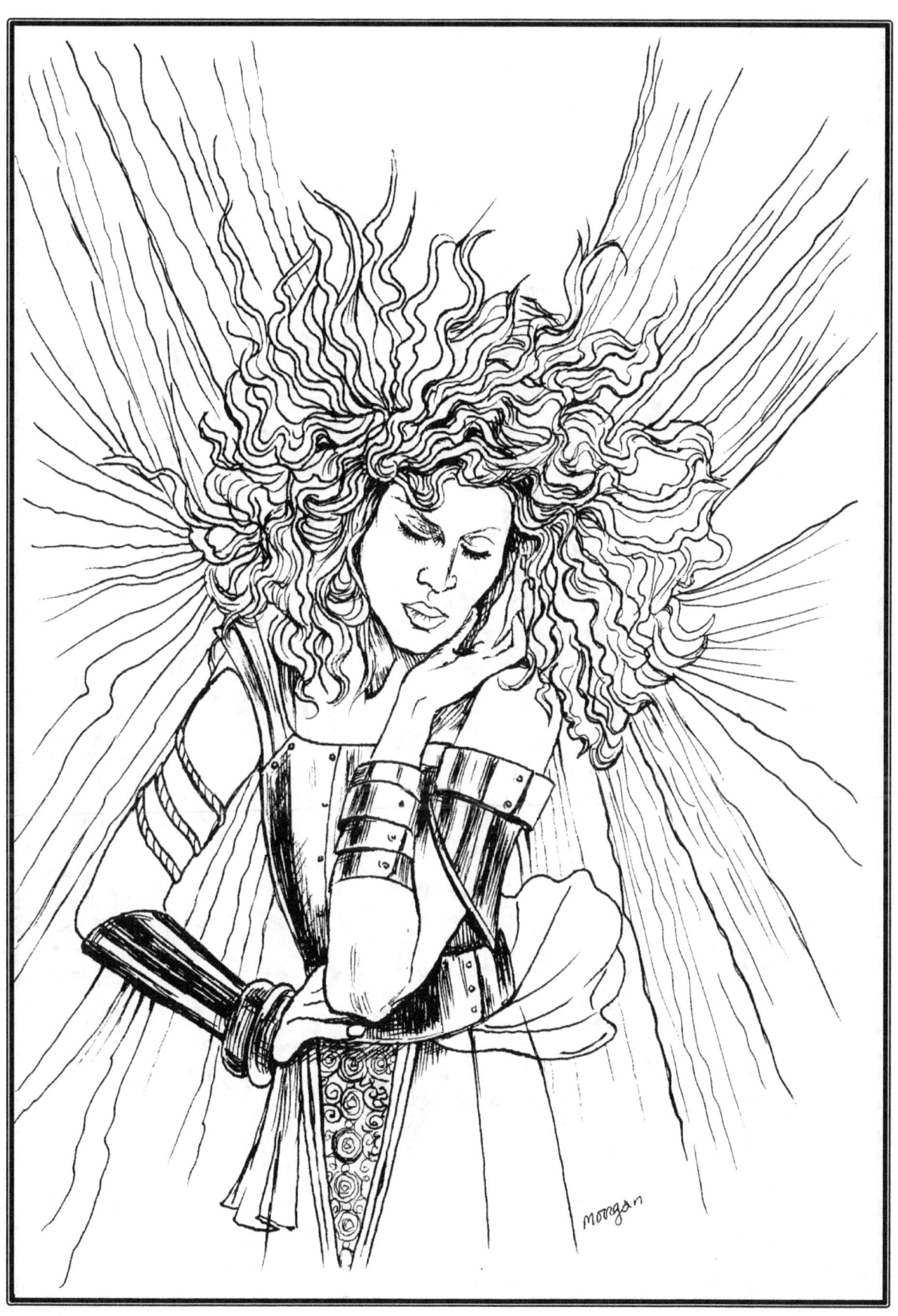

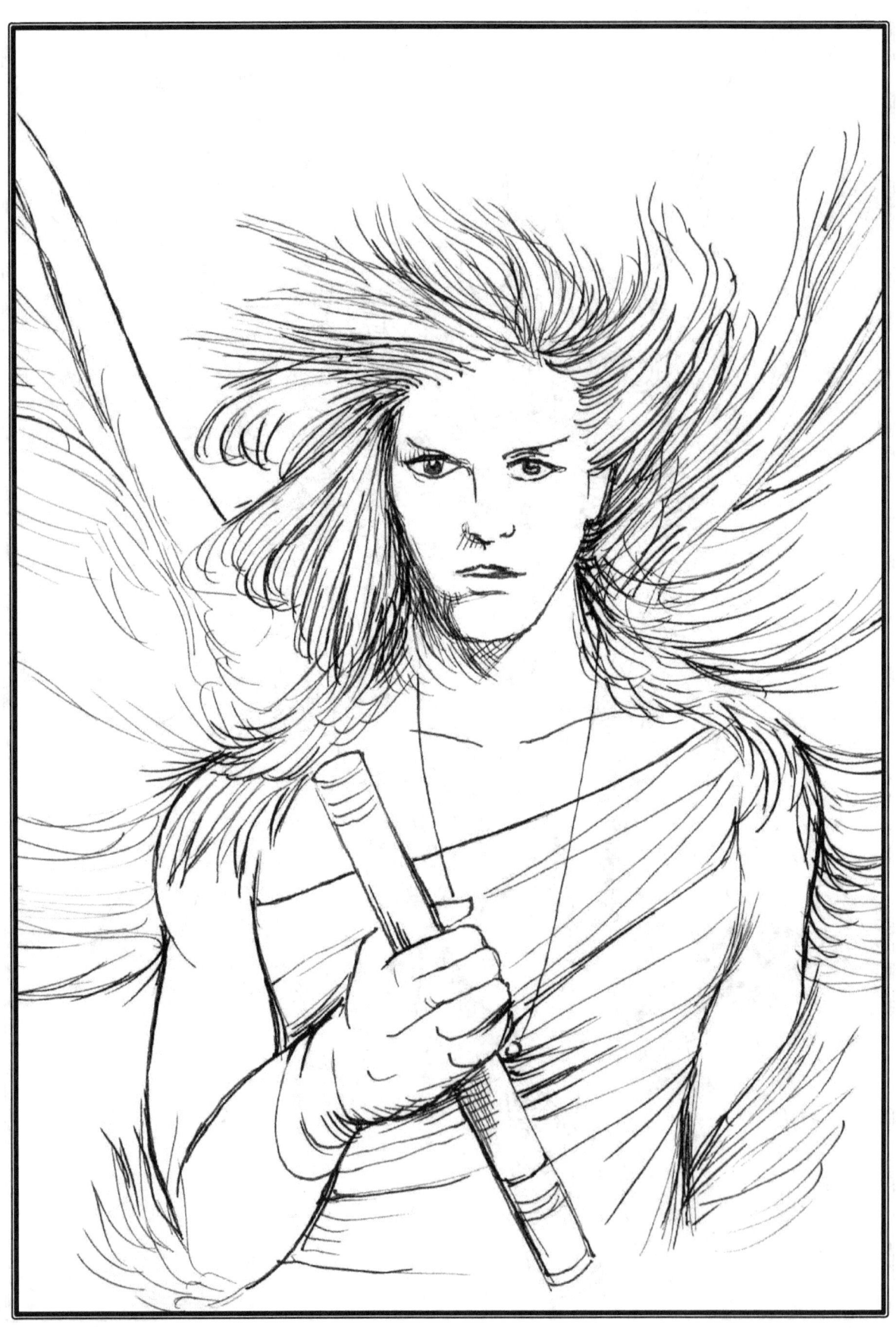

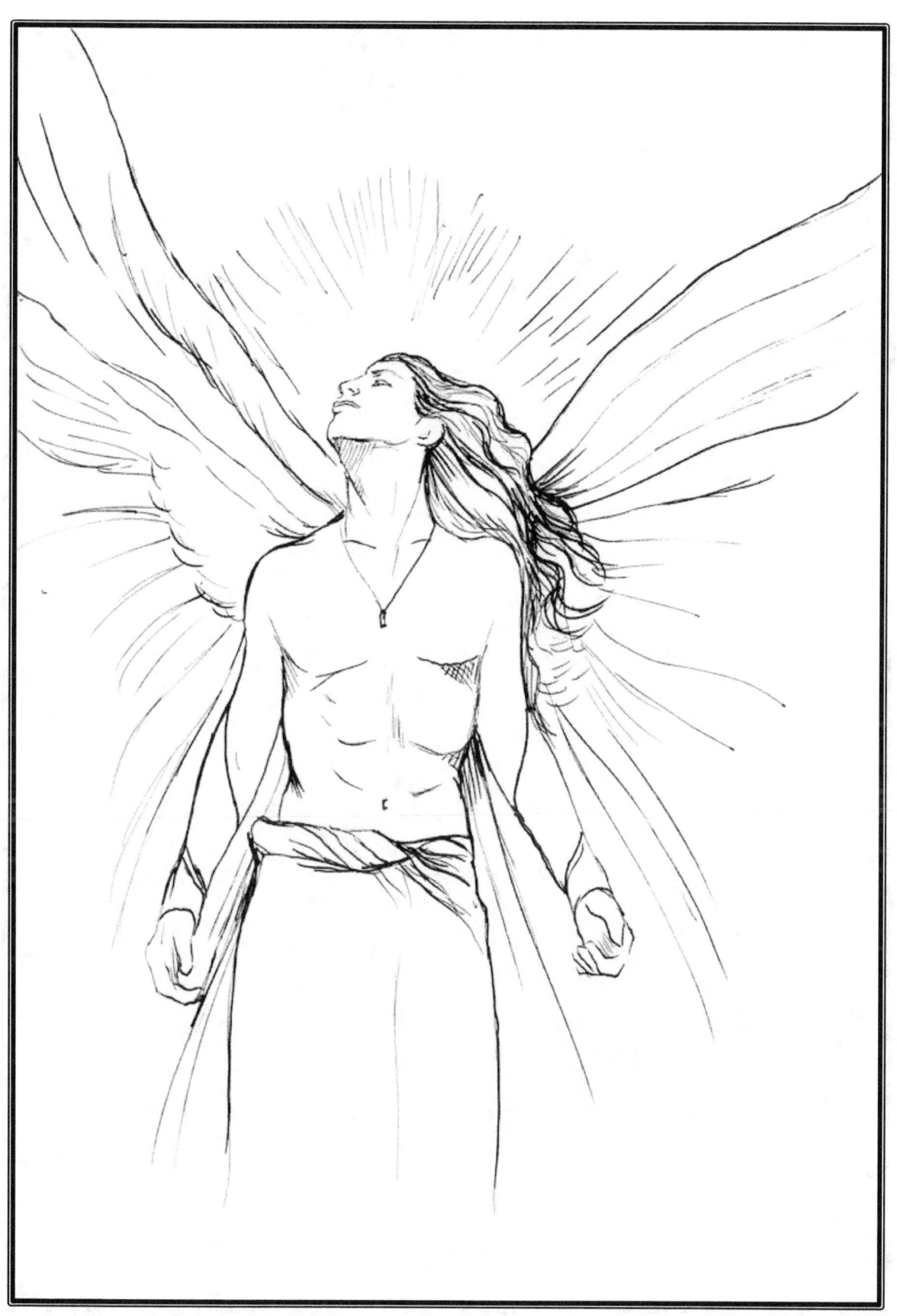

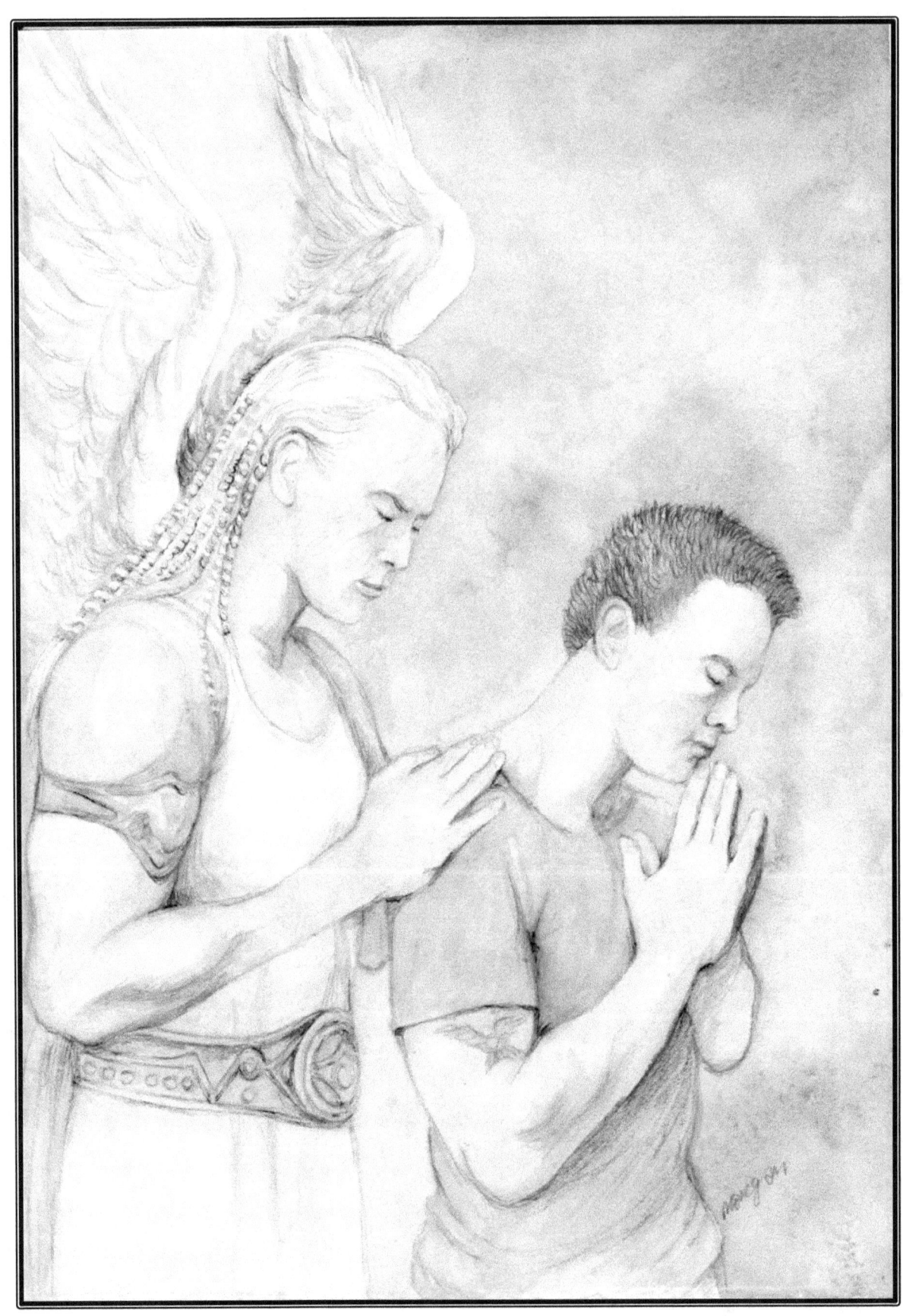

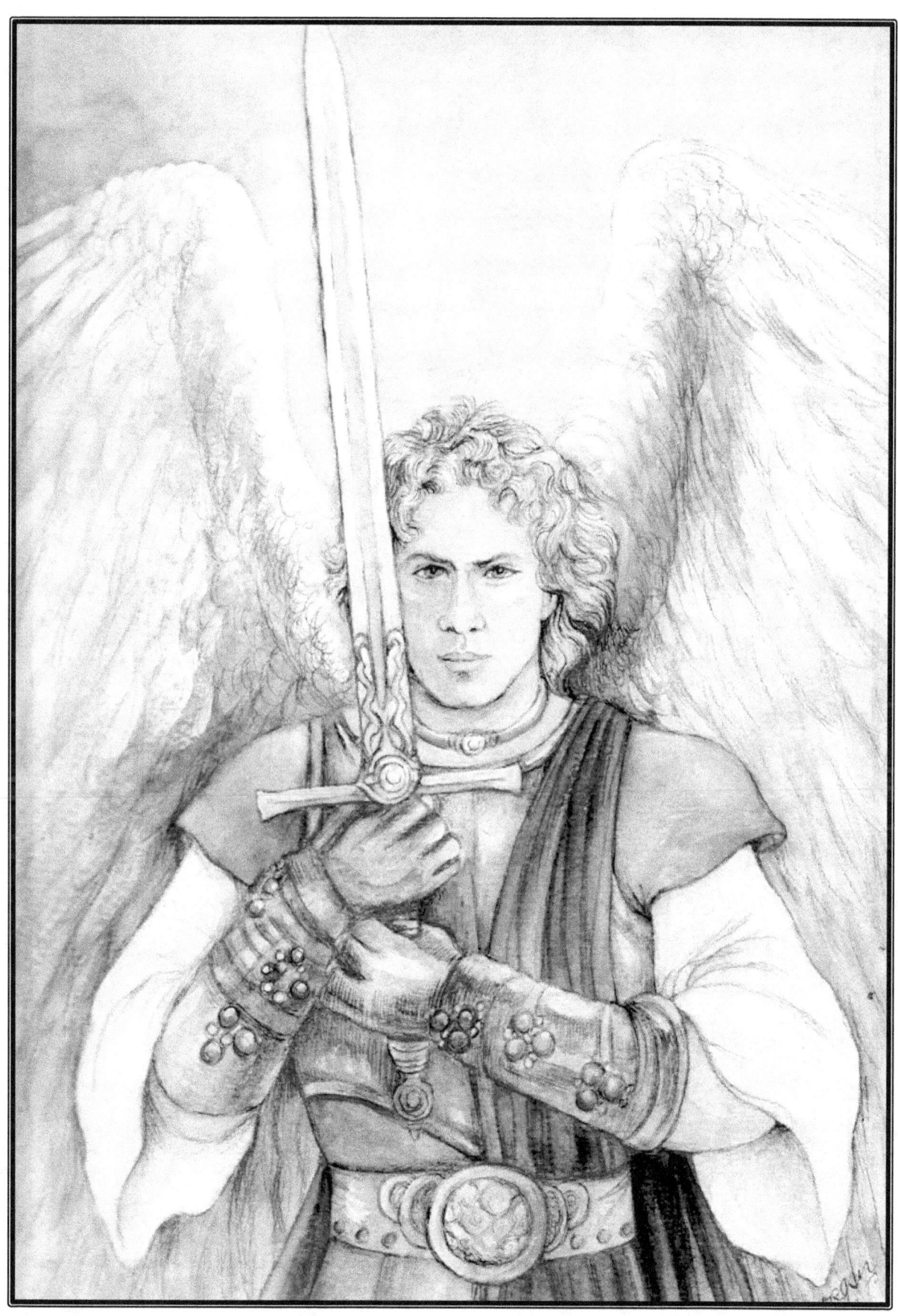

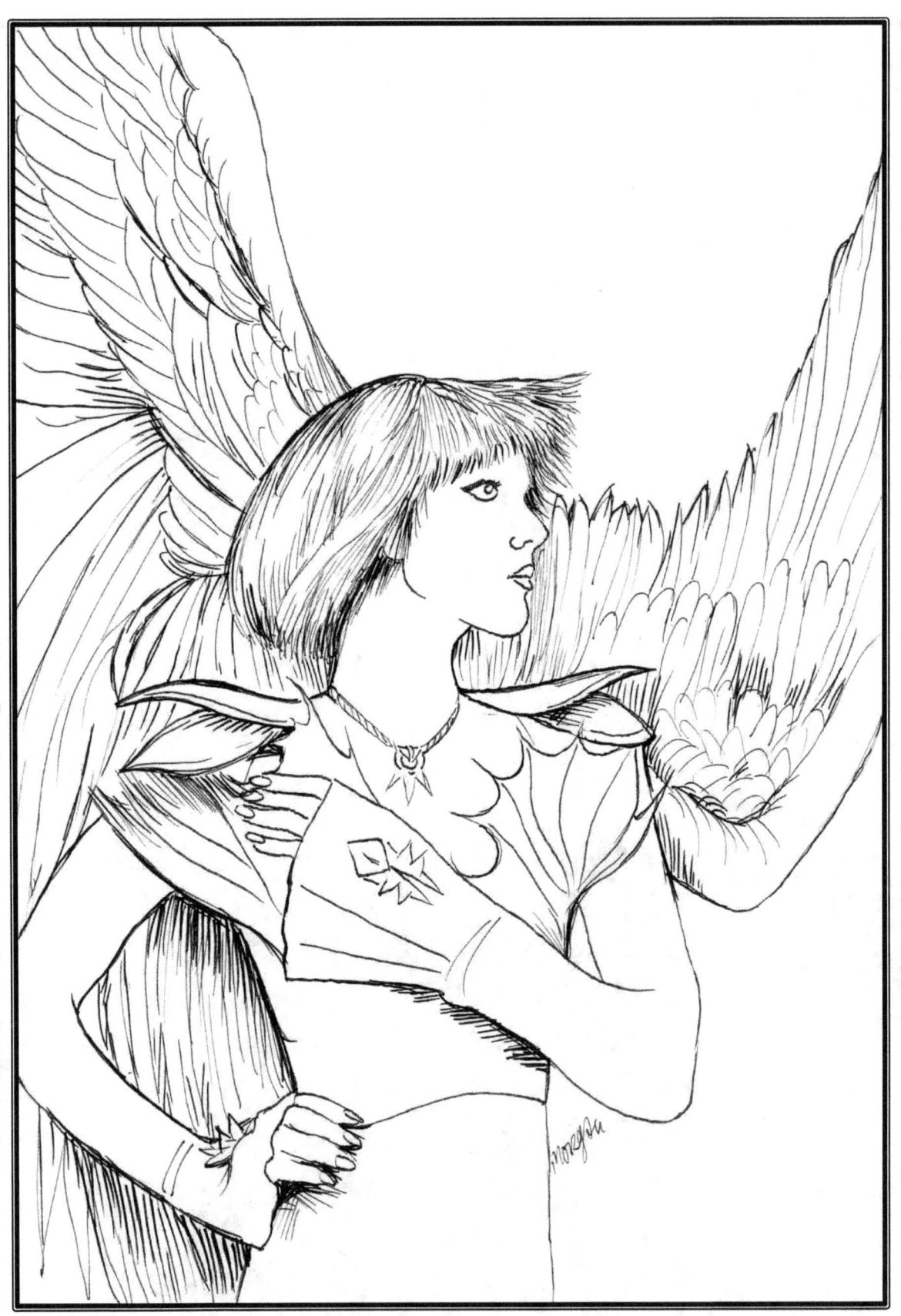

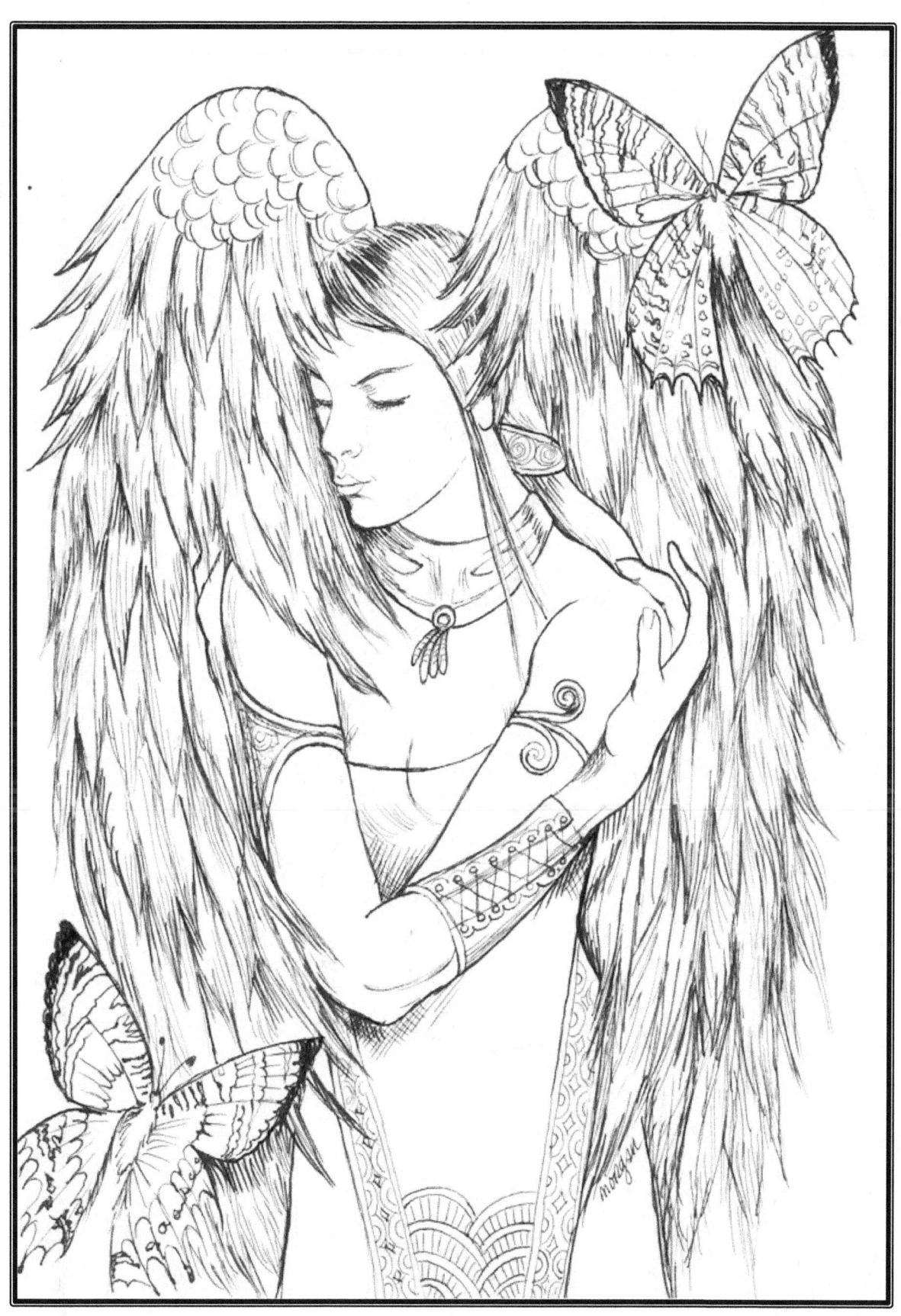

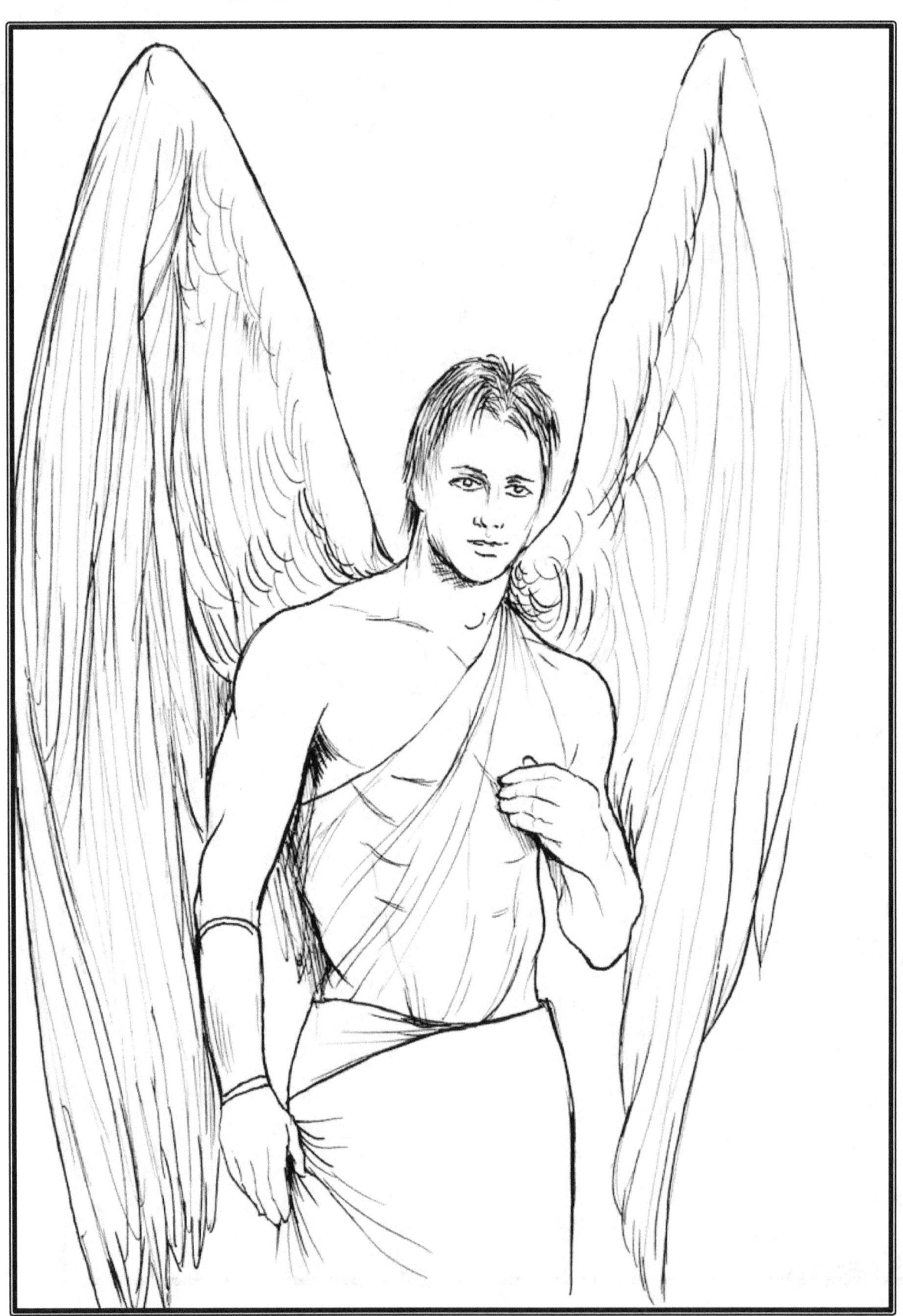

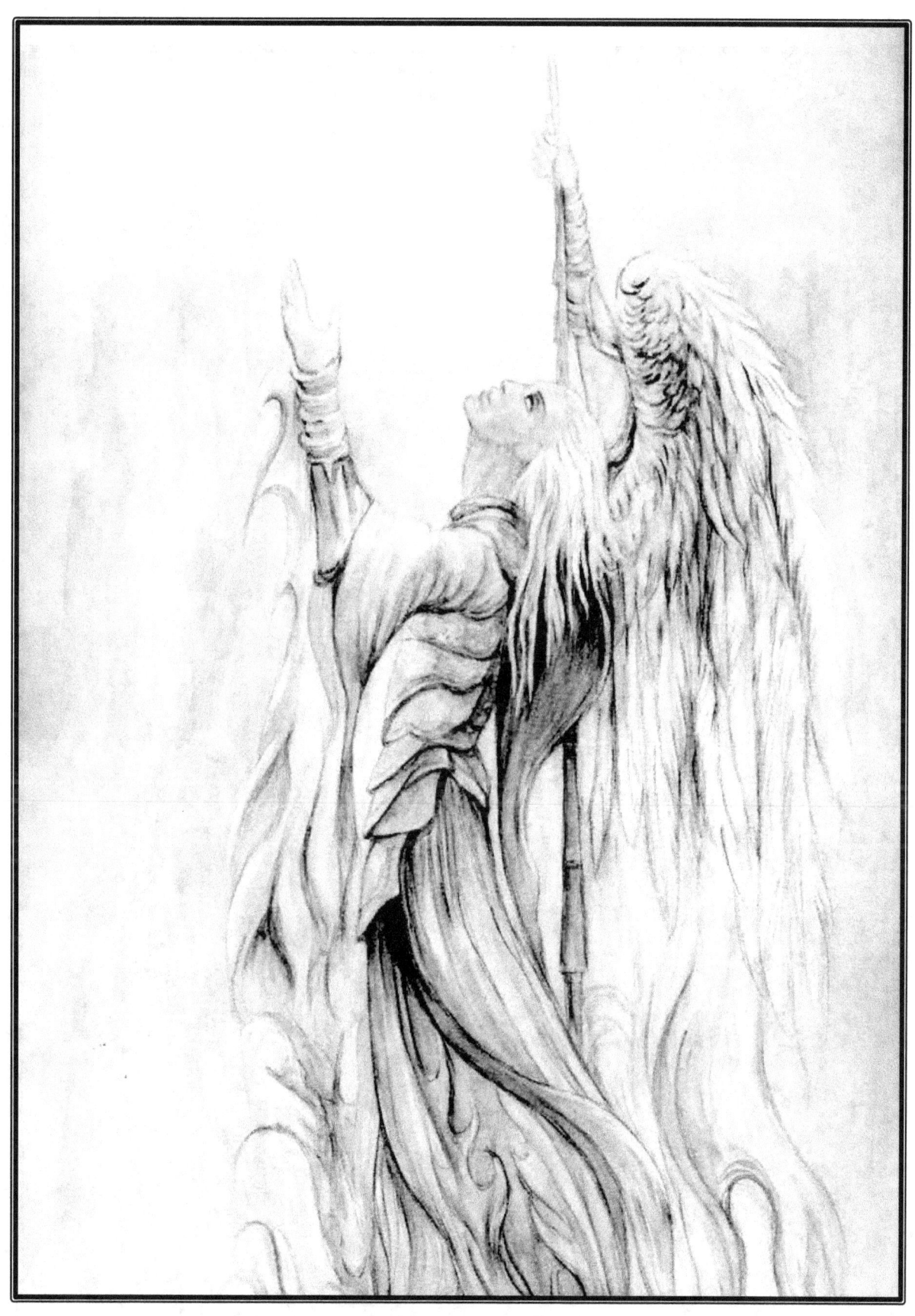

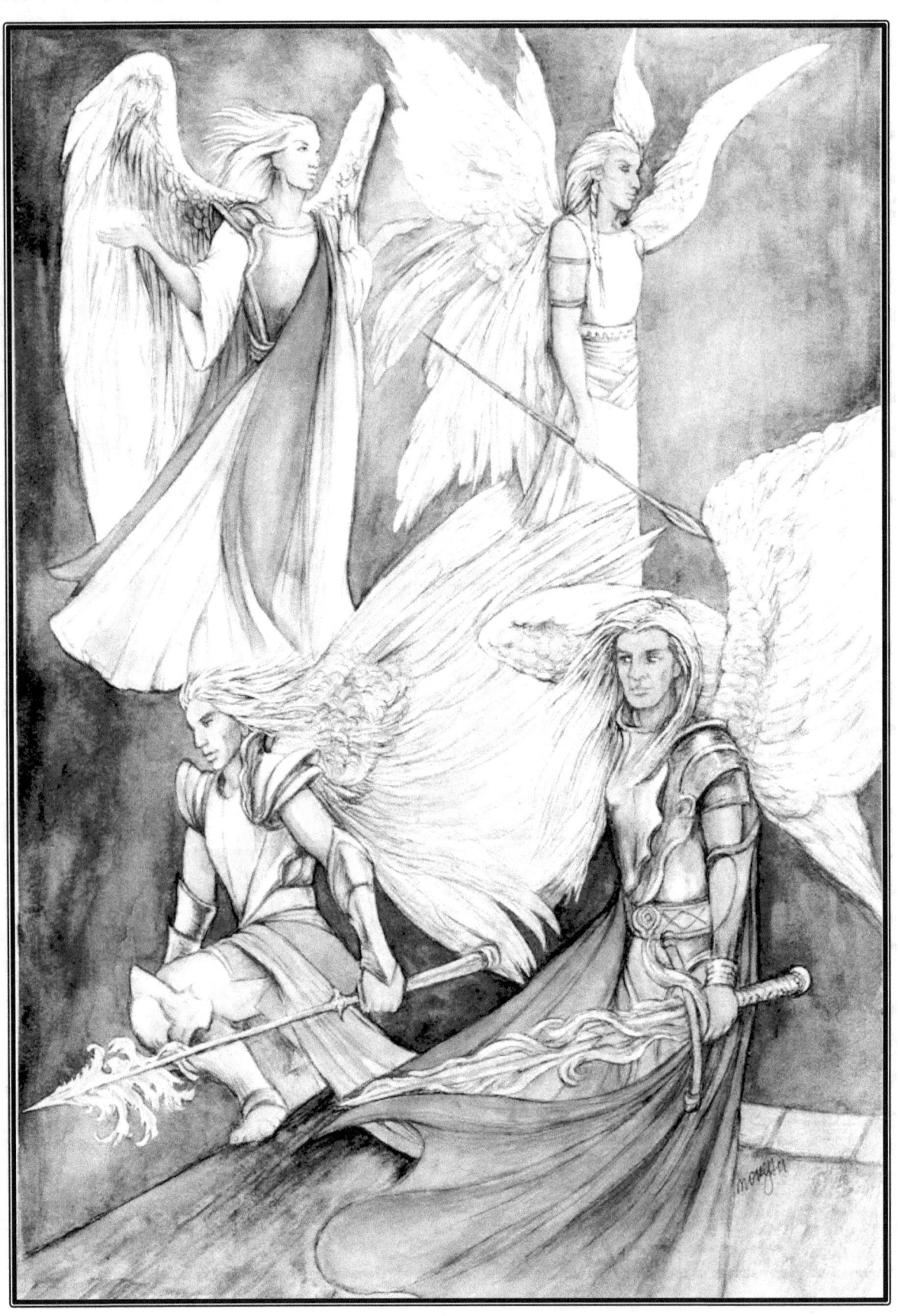